Bon Voyage

Time for Travel

# PACKING CHECKLIST

DATE OF TRIP: _____   DURATION: _____

TRAVEL BUCKET LIST

PLACES I WANT TO VISIT:

THINGS I WANT TO SEE:

TOP 3 DESTINATIONS:

MY TRAVEL JOURNAL

DATE:

WHAT I DID TODAY

HIGHLIGHT OF THE DAY

TRAVEL SNAPSHOT

DOODLES

MY TRAVEL JOURNAL

DATE:

WHAT I DID TODAY

HIGHLIGHT OF THE DAY

TRAVEL SNAPSHOT

DOODLES

MY TRAVEL JOURNAL

DATE:

WHAT I DID TODAY

HIGHLIGHT OF THE DAY

TRAVEL SNAPSHOT

DOODLES

MY TRAVEL JOURNAL

DATE:

WHAT I DID TODAY

HIGHLIGHT OF THE DAY

TRAVEL SNAPSHOT

DOODLES

MY TRAVEL JOURNAL

DATE:

WHAT I DID TODAY

HIGHLIGHT OF THE DAY

TRAVEL SNAPSHOT

DOODLES

MY TRAVEL JOURNAL

DATE:

WHAT I DID TODAY

HIGHLIGHT OF THE DAY

TRAVEL SNAPSHOT

DOODLES

MY TRAVEL JOURNAL

DATE:

WHAT I DID TODAY

HIGHLIGHT OF THE DAY

TRAVEL SNAPSHOT

DOODLES

MY TRAVEL JOURNAL

DATE:

WHAT I DID TODAY

HIGHLIGHT OF THE DAY

TRAVEL SNAPSHOT

DOODLES

MY TRAVEL JOURNAL

DATE:

WHAT I DID TODAY

HIGHLIGHT OF THE DAY

TRAVEL SNAPSHOT

DOODLES

MY TRAVEL JOURNAL

DATE:

WHAT I DID TODAY

HIGHLIGHT OF THE DAY

TRAVEL SNAPSHOT

DOODLES

MY TRAVEL JOURNAL

DATE:

WHAT I DID TODAY

HIGHLIGHT OF THE DAY

TRAVEL SNAPSHOT

DOODLES

MY TRAVEL JOURNAL

DATE:

WHAT I DID TODAY

HIGHLIGHT OF THE DAY

TRAVEL SNAPSHOT

DOODLES

MY TRAVEL JOURNAL

DATE:

WHAT I DID TODAY

HIGHLIGHT OF THE DAY

TRAVEL SNAPSHOT

DOODLES

MY TRAVEL JOURNAL

DATE:

WHAT I DID TODAY

HIGHLIGHT OF THE DAY

TRAVEL SNAPSHOT

DOODLES

MY TRAVEL JOURNAL

DATE:

WHAT I DID TODAY

HIGHLIGHT OF THE DAY

TRAVEL SNAPSHOT

DOODLES

MY TRAVEL JOURNAL

DATE:

WHAT I DID TODAY

HIGHLIGHT OF THE DAY

TRAVEL SNAPSHOT

DOODLES

MY TRAVEL JOURNAL

DATE:

WHAT I DID TODAY

HIGHLIGHT OF THE DAY

TRAVEL SNAPSHOT

DOODLES

MY TRAVEL JOURNAL

DATE:

WHAT I DID TODAY

HIGHLIGHT OF THE DAY

TRAVEL SNAPSHOT

DOODLES

MY TRAVEL JOURNAL

DATE:

WHAT I DID TODAY

HIGHLIGHT OF THE DAY

TRAVEL SNAPSHOT

DOODLES

MY TRAVEL JOURNAL

DATE:

WHAT I DID TODAY

HIGHLIGHT OF THE DAY

TRAVEL SNAPSHOT

DOODLES

MY TRAVEL JOURNAL

DATE:

WHAT I DID TODAY

HIGHLIGHT OF THE DAY

TRAVEL SNAPSHOT

DOODLES

MY TRAVEL JOURNAL

DATE:

WHAT I DID TODAY

HIGHLIGHT OF THE DAY

TRAVEL SNAPSHOT

DOODLES

MY TRAVEL JOURNAL

DATE:

WHAT I DID TODAY

HIGHLIGHT OF THE DAY

TRAVEL SNAPSHOT

DOODLES

MY TRAVEL JOURNAL

DATE:

WHAT I DID TODAY

HIGHLIGHT OF THE DAY

TRAVEL SNAPSHOT

DOODLES

Made in the USA
Las Vegas, NV
13 December 2021